BLOODSTONE COWBOY

KARA JACKSON

Haymarket Books
Chicago, IL

Published in 2019 by
Haymarket Books
P.O. Box 180165
Chicago, IL 60618
773-583-7884
www.haymarketbooks.org
info@haymarketbooks.org

ISBN: 978-1-64259-120-0

Distributed to the trade in the US through Consortium Book Sales and
Distribution (www.cbsd.com) and internationally through Ingram Publisher
Services International (www.ingramcontent.com).

This book was published with the generous support of Lannan Foundation
and Wallace Action Fund.

Cover artwork by Sarah Lotus.
Text design by Jamie Kerry.

Library of Congress Cataloging-in-Publication data is available.

10 9 8 7 6 5 4 3 2

The BreakBeat Poets series

ABOUT THE BREAKBEAT POETS SERIES

The BreakBeat Poets series, curated by Kevin Coval and Nate Marshall, is committed to work that brings the aesthetic of hip-hop practice to the page. These books are a cipher for the fresh, with an eye always to the next. We strive to center and showcase some of the most exciting voices in literature, art, and culture.

BREAKBEAT POETS SERIES TITLES INCLUDE:

The BreakBeat Poets: New American Poetry in the Age of Hip-Hop, edited by Kevin Coval, Quraysh Ali Lansana, and Nate Marshall

This Is Modern Art: A Play, Idris Goodwin and Kevin Coval

The Breakbeat Poets Vol. 2: Black Girl Magic, edited by Mahogany L. Browne, Jamila Woods, and Idrissa Simmonds

Human Highlight, Idris Goodwin and Kevin Coval

On My Way to Liberation, H. Melt

Black Queer Hoe, Britteney Black Rose Kapri

Citizen Illegal, José Olivarez

Milwaukee Avenue, Kevin Coval

The BreakBeat Poets Vol. 3: Halal if You Hear Me, edited by Fatimah Asghar and Safia Elhillo

Commando, E'mon Lauren

Graphite, Patricia Frazier

Everything Must Go, Kevin Coval

contents.

my virginity signed a bad contract

victim of the same debt
rappers go on TV to talk about
my virginity started to keep money under her mattress
asked neighbors for quarters to finish her laundry

last week someone tried to tow my virginity's car
but she had something on the guy. he let her off
& still called her a slippery bitch before backing up
into oncoming traffic so my virginity started taking the bus
or caught the green line towards harlem

my virginity calls her mother to say she's staying out
of trouble *hell maybe i'll start going to church with you ma*
my virginity would say but never abandons the sermon
of half of her joint, settles by telling mama *christmas*

my virginity is trying to work out
more my virginity sets three alarms to wake up
in 30 minute increments but sleeps
through all of them

happier elsewhere

after Denise Duhamel

my virginity is somewhere eating a greasy burger
with extra mustard. when i told my mother she held me real

tight and told me about a bad man who used to kiss her before
my father did. we put up signs for my virginity, waited for it

to come home like a cat. i walked around shaking a can
of its favorite food. *have you seen it? have you seen it?*

i smelled the coats of men hoping my sex rose
from their pockets. when they asked me what it looked like,

i could only say *far away*. it's easy to think of my virginity
dancing the cowboy cha cha. it's easy to think it's happier

elsewhere, shaking its hips into a far away wind.

on my birth name

1

my name was supposed to be stuffed in a mouth
a tobacco so thick the letters smell

my name is a white woman
waiting for   a rescue,
some cadillac for her to stretch out on

i have been given a pricey cigarette name
that sounds good
over phone calls   a bright sneaker name

people have tried to call me
someone wrong   they have called
the wrong person in me, let a car engine sit
in the oil of my wrong name
cara is a vehicle running through me

a bad toss of my name
a tangerine rightfully orange
this strange citrus i answer to

because my right name is too short
to argue over, four letters
not worth making food of

what is this fire
we are counting on? when did tobacco
not do the trick of weaving something blacker

than our own mouths?

2

where is my joke name?
every country girl's right to be called something   silly

Monica called Jerry
Debra called Mickey
Carrie called Didt

our blood   is a punchline we defend

i want to be a joke too
i want my name to never stop knocking
to ask   who's there?

and stick its tongue out

first

the women in my family have bones in the right places. bridges on
their cheeks, structures of caution where the fat might get in. i am
the daughter with the round face. the women in my family have
noses like compasses, each sniff a sharp indication of home. Carrie
is old now, but a young woman sits in her face, like a bug trapped
between glass. Bernie, who burrows like a Cherokee rose, Debra's
bones, firm in their residence, face permanent as a coffin. the wom-
en in my family are so beautiful, they don't have to use their bodies.
they get two bags of flour for the price of their jaws, scam grandpa
out of the last of his taxi money. my mother's face is a disco whistle
that moves my father for catfish, for pine nuts, for the remote.

i am the first ugly woman spun out of this blood.
where is my asking chin?
what will they make of my age?
what shape will they give my face?
will my bones be arranged on a page?
is there a young woman sitting in me
 ready to make orders?
if my daughter writes poems,
will she make a flower of me?

anthem for my belly after eating too much

i look in the mirror, and all the chips i've eaten
this month have accumulated
like schoolwork, at the bottom of my tummy
my belly, a country i'm trying to love.
my mouth is a lover devoted to you,
my belly, my belly
the birds will string a song together
with wind for you and your army
of solids, militia of grease.
americans love excess, but we also love jeans,
and refuse to make excess comfortable in them.
i step into a fashionable prison,
my middle managed and fastened into
suffering. my gracious gut,
dutiful dome, i will wear a house for you
that you can live in, promise walls
that embrace your growing flesh,
and watch you reach towards everything possible.

mean streak

i want to be as threatening as beet juice
to a clean white, threatening as a sharp wind
to a shown ankle. i want people to pay to see me

like a horror movie, fear prepared in their pockets.
i want to be more threatening than a red notice on an envelope.
when i speak, i want my mouth attached to a warning,

like a small thing that can be swallowed
i want to threaten the way fat does
a button, hips filling my jeans like ammo.

Grandma Thelma wears her mean like a girdle.
my mother says i'm almost as mean as her,
that my mean grows as a streak in my hair.

God, make me as mean as Thelma
give me a mean i can hide behind,
a mean that fastens me into a dress,

a mean i'll pull out of my drawer
let the mean conquer my hair,
like troops poking for surrender

and then, grow to my ankles
even the ants will see the steam.

moonshine speaks

i am a planet, a liquid jupiter
y'all find under the bed
what good is your belly if not shaking
with something illegal
what good is the ra ra ra ra ra ra
ra ra ra ra ra ra ra rockin ra ra rockin' roll blues
how many hymns can you sing
without looking down
it's true! what they say about your brass-lipped uncle
it's true! the monsters under this country are real
burn on the way down, are homemade

the boogie man made a bet with a banshee
to see who could hold the most false water
then run up the street without hacking it up
both of them fell in the dirt
and gave the porch folk a good laugh
the kind that gives them more years
to drink and to make drink
untasty things get the earth moving

country boys are no good so why are you
trying to drink wine with a cursive name
the grumble of your grandpa's many stomachs
is not French, it's just me

you have rivers of me to sell
your blood is an economy of me
there's no Riesling waiting to claim you
no gin and tonic flavored hustle

a country boy is bad for trying to forget
the blood that runs with something
that knows his true name

are you good   and country   and free
or just drunk

in defense of chitlins

don't you still hold the lover
when he comes home smelling of work
won't you hold your nose for that someone

sleeping next to you   wouldn't you
still fold yourself into this stinky thing
if he were heading for the steam
if the loofa were lathered,
if his hands clawed to get clean

if he would return tender
as the middle of anything   wouldn't you
still offer your mouth as some prize

some forgiveness for assuming
beloved things smell good
for not understanding some beauty
must stink first

this funk feeds people
this must makes meals
praise the whiff that waters mouths

what brings skunk wives to their husbands
moves beetles to fuck

and me to this pot

blood is not a woman's currency

i face mother nature like rent, dweller of my routine faucet.
we get along like languages that are similar.
sometimes, i can find something in my blood
that's recognizable, sometimes i find myself
in that timely pond, but it doesn't make me a woman.

when asked of my kind i wouldn't show my blood
my hands maybe, the way my fingers find homes
in my temples, or the uncertainty of my teeth.

everyone bleeds but not everyone can exchange their blood
for whole countries. it's true, blood is a currency
for someone with too much
power. blood a dollar in the right hands.

the world is about to end and
my grandparents are in love

still, living like they orbit one another
my grandfather, the planet & grandma his moon assigned
by some gravitational pull. they have loved long enough,
for a working man to retire. grandma says she's not tired,

she wears her husband like a coat that survives every season,
talks about him the way my parents talk about vinyl
the subject salvaged by the tent of their tongues.
grandma returns to her love like a hymn, marks it with a color.

when the world ends will it suck the earth of all its love?
will i go taking somebody's hand
my skin becoming their skin?
the digital age is taking away our winters,

and i'm afraid the sun is my soulmate,
that waste waits for a wet kiss
carbon calls me pretty and i think
death is a good first date.

i hope when the world ends it leaves them be,
spares grandpa and his game,
grandma spinning corn into weight,

the two of them, reeling into western
theme songs, the TV louder
than whatever's coming.

love poem with a knife

in talking about loving you, i consider murder.
consider your pistol of a mouth, jaw long and smoking.

when i ask how to be pretty for you, you suggest murder.
defend it, call a dead woman the least vain. in talking
about loving men, my mother suggests loving a knife

first. learn if sharpness can be a good father, if a blade can make
kissy faces. every woman wants a man, few want a good knife.
i name my kitchen a love war, look for you in the cutting drawer,

look for you in my razor. make a romance
out of nicking. i have no secrets for first dates,
just keeping chopping. put his edge to your neck.

he will let you bleed first (no, after you). and this is why i leave
and come back. i know i'm a woman, by the way i take
war, by the way i let weapons give me children, even sliced and
undone,

by the way our love is pressing the wound.

landays from the woman who pulled her pepper spray out on the CTA:

boys do not know fire like my squeeze.
fool, i hope you undress the red how you undress me.

guns are not cute and sold at Walgreens.
men always use bullets to get a hello from me.

an eye for an eye, a husband's tale.
i give an eye to keep my body and keep it well.

if i yell fire, i mean to yell you.
sometimes a fire is a rough man who needs a wife too.

on the red line, a man slit a throat.
as they filmed, he licked the blood of a girl who said no.

you told me my no can't stop your eyes.
so my no became an evil chemical. surprise, surprise.

on beating your ass

if you expect god to take you
quietly if you do the dishes and try to

drown if you wear pants that make a man
want to wear you if you drink soda

in the dark if you grab in the refrigerator without
permission if you wear eyeshadow

you can see through if you bring a boy
in here who we can't see

if you wear your hair long enough for him
to get lost in if you drink without looking

first to see the colors mix if your keys aren't out
and sharp if you wear too much

oil (men can't resist slick) if you scratch
what itches if he hits

and you don't leave him if he kiss and you
cry if you say he's fine

if you drop your teddy bear if you burn the
doll house if you break

the doll and give her to me to fix if you run
out the house without shoes

or your brother if you walk with headphones
in. if you walk with a switch.

if you get kidnapped and they bring you
back if you say a prayer to me

after i'm good and dead if you bleed your
blood and don't scab

if you bite your nails if you unfold your
clothes if you sleep

naked in your room if you shave
and distribute your smooth

if you think god can handle your loud
if you don't take your body with you

i'm going to need a bigger belt
to save you

tribute for when i'm quiet

quiet is a mouth i screw onto my mouth
quiet, a twin spinning my evil
quiet, a snake i hold without flinching
i treat my quiet like a pocket knife
quiet, a blade i sharpen and consider
ready my quiet for any jaw
quiet, a suspect i bring into questioning
quiet, a fire i use for cooking
quiet, this country i defend
quiet, a law i have written
quiet, so i am told by every man
who will surely kill me
quiet prayer in the mouth of all my victims
i am so quiet
mice make a simile out of me

things the toilet borrowed

old teeth, brass sections of digested sound, cranberry juice, lost
hairs, thanksgiving dinners, villages of devoured things, missed
diseases, the milk of funerals, snatched pearls, swallowed tears,
rocks from mars, glitter, fun that started as a fire in my throat, the
night blended into slime, the guilt grease makes, boogers, mud
from the rio grande, iron, beet juice, bright blood, the possibility of
names, an answer to a false equation, cobwebs, the sun confronted
by something brighter than itself, birth charts, photo ink, toenails,
aglets, all the smooth of a limb that has never been touched

        * * *

do not give something a name,
if you cannot hear its cough and the breath that follows.

do not give something a name when you know the earth
is searching for names, history a mouth begging

for syllables to suck on. history is hungry
for the soft bones of the possible,

starves for something to go wrong
in the tunnels of many.

        * * *

we wouldn't even have names if we didn't find them on graves.
someone has to die for someone to be called my name.
i was born because of a cold sentence, parting signature, stone cold
autograph.
i know i was named after someone dead and someone who's death i
have written down.

* * *

i sat on the john and filtered my river for names, thought i had
caught something
in the warm glittering oil of me, but the toilet, like history, wants
names
in the hat of someone who begs, tricks the dead into a cold broth of
loss.

* * *

and i am a machine who handles error
i sat on the john and it handled me,
baptized my fiction and when i piss now,
i look for someone who would only recognize me.

methods for catching the sun

sometimes i listen to the music we only listen to in the summer
to call the sun in, sometimes i have to make the sun from scratch,

write it like the tooth fairy, schedule its fiction.
the imagination tricks children into believing false givers,

the sun fools me into living, the morning one of its best jokes.
i sharpen the sun and run it through my face like a family tale,

passed down and claiming a hole in me.
i believe the sun is the first lover to leave

me waiting, a glowing promise the day leaves
like a kiss that shakes me out of bed.

sometimes i charm the sun into making
its commute, light a route over my cheek,

i tickle its orbit with the hair of my words,
make it rise out of flattery.

does the sun have ears it is dying to glitter?
maybe i'll toss it a family recipe,

bribe it with biscuits,
coax it with cornstarch.

maybe the sun will rise out of oil,
change color with the onions.

i'm going to need something that'll make it stay
jail it to its place, divorce it from descending.

oh, sun, be as permanent as suffering
as lasting as what wounds.

Maya grows on a tree every year when the season is right

she announces herself as a fruit, reddened and relearning its color. we talk about death like a dead person doesn't always outlive themselves in being dead, as in someday we will be 50 and we will not remember what brought us together in the first place, as in someday i will forgive myself for every assignment i didn't turn in after the news. when we found out teenagers could die, it was in honors french class. we read Dead Maya in the glow of our palms. we slid Dead Maya into our pockets for safe keeping. now the Maya we knew as alive is lost in some kind of short memory, but the idea of her being dead swells and softens in our hands. the mystery of cancer is a bitter sugar. we pick our dead homies off of a vine and check them for bruises. we stay alive a little longer in the name of all the poems we will write about them. and i know the fruit metaphor gives me closure. i know that grief makes me smelly. i know that writing a poem forgives the shower water that doesn't run, the paper that goes unwritten, the pile of homework that announces itself like a fruit falling. all of my friends who are dead are also ripe. they are all fresh produce. they are all sweet in the center. all my friends who are dead have patted me on the back for getting through high school. it's hard to believe honor roll can make room for grief. my college list means so much more, because Maya always wanted to go to the east coast. and to say i graduated is also to say the tumor didn't win. the tumor is never stronger than the best friend. the tumor couldn't take me even if it wore boxing gloves, even if it fought professionally on tv. there's a cheering section in heaven where Maya stands swinging a pom-pom; a tree moving its head with the wind.

lost & found

i thought i left my black in a safe
place i thought my black pulled on me,
an umbilical cord, thought my black was cut
for safekeeping. i thought my black was floating
in a jar, or maybe my black is a button
i'm supposed to rush to in case of emergency.
i take my black off of my shoulders and hang it up
my father only mentions his black if he's drunk.
my black is something we claim
on our taxes, the very high ones, my friends
they come to visit and ask me how i've gotten on
without it, ask do i miss my black
like a childhood pet? i tell them it's around
here somewhere, dust assigned to some crevice,
sock in the lost & found. i ask my neighbors
if they've seen my black and they call me
a nigger
how did they find it so quickly?
like a bird heard and recognized.

poem for the midwest

my american wasteland. you sick, twisted blade of grass.
your kisses are not real, they were just the wind.

your hedonism is below zero. i don't think i love you,
just the fact that you let me smoke

in your closet. you make my nose red, and do not come
to collect my blood. you make me wear three sweaters

just to hug my friends. your summers are a false
honeymoons. i fall for your sun every time,

but i don't abandon my coat. it is brown
and it is sitting there in the den, like a dog

that just heard people outside. i am afraid to leave you
and your tricky weather. i am afraid because my mother

makes good potatoes with spinach, my father knows
how to keep wrinkles out of the laundry,

and i am a mess who is calling herself an adult,
and you are the toughest girl i have ever sort of loved.

a case for long johns

after José Olivarez

psychology says body temperature is determined
by the way you have been held.
america is no hug, no rock and jostle
my mother settles blankets over me like she is hiding
a spare key. dad gets new gloves every year.
we say white people are crazy in our long underwear,
watch the consequence of a certain caress.
these white boys wear shorts like hunted skins,
show they have more by wearing less.
i used to wish i was more durable in the cold
but i know glass needs heat to harden.

white girl victory & other american myths

history does not come in cereal boxes.
you cannot try it in different flavors like lip balm.
no blood with the taste of coconut breeze,
no pistol will make a cherry red out of me.

your hair is confused,
a beetle turned on its back,
a dog seized by the invisible joke of hands,
a coin tossed that does not fall.

when blood dries it leaves villages, ghosts
the women you bump in the street,
girls you wear as savior caps,
mamas with tobacco in their spit,
they will return on your pavement,
crimson little kingdoms they'll make.
you suffer their red forces.

you thought this country deserved your hair,
which is really a spider
a child's fear, a colonial beast
the venom sits on the top of your head

america is a bloody pastime,
a brutal arcade, its buttons of wonder
set to kill me, and you think the war was fought
over your ponytail.
who was the fool that made gold out of your head?
and did they know none of you can be gold if not stolen.

america, a salt bath for my mother's feet
america, cheap fling in the night

america, my poison of choice
america, land of my teeth.

ode to pretty when i was ugly before

i grew into my big mouth so well,
people address it as Miss Big Mouth,
put out their hands for a chance of her graze.

i grew into my destructive elbows,
have accepted their blades, the messes they make.
i fill in my chin well now, like a glove.

i admit my fashion is crooked,
but if it didn't look good,
ski trails wouldn't trace after my jaw,
wouldn't carve my name into foothills
people wouldn't die trying to ride down my face.

my hair is so blue it moves people,
like a fish moves toward something made for its mouth.
i've made old ladies cry with my hair,
painters follow me home,
picasso tried to size up my skull
but i'm not fond of his blue period.

i think sad things sparkle more than they dull.
i've found the saddest things with bows attached,
get sad under the highest sun.
in fact, i grew into my sad too, so now
people ask me where i got it from,
start eyeing my sad for a brand attached to it.
i've considered putting my sad into jars and distributing it,
some kind of home liquor i'll whip up.

i changed my hair because change is a sad thing
if you aren't the one making it.

i don't know if i'm pretty,
i just know i was ugly before,
the way a war is ugly
to the ones doing the welcoming home.

i woke up and the day caught me

in its mouth like a strand of yarn
i am useful
the motivation for a scarf, maybe

some stitch started to be finished
i will make up someone's
heat i will be a fire
so intricate it can be worn

i woke up and the day called on me
specifically, threw my name through the sky
the way children are thought up
trials pulled through the stars

i woke up and like anyone who wakes
and asks why i checked my feet,
rubbed the bones for their reality
i keep waking though i've asked for rest

cornered the moon in the alley,
pawned the dark to assume its place
and still i return to that burning chin
honor that persistent candle

because who will wake up if not me?
who will the day catch then
if i am not the center of its tongue?

what of the women who keep waking?
what of my mother, who has asked for rest, too?
and her mother, tucked into an endless slumber

i woke up and the day thanked me
for coming so far. i know rest is a long
walk from the sun, i know we've been up
for so long, that sleep doesn't settle
for my blood. me, daughter of the rooster's song

but when the day calls i will answer to my name
claim it like a fire rushing toward living things
i will rise   because there is someone praying
for me to remain still

acknowledgments

Giant thanks to Frontier Poetry for first publishing "love poem with a knife" and Third Coast Magazine for publishing "lost & found".

I want to thank my bloodline. Thank you to my family. Thank you to the women who raised me. To Ms.Little, my second mother. Thank you to my big brother Forrest.

To Sarah Lotus for doing the amazing cover art!

Thank you Peter Kahn for making me write poetry.

To the ones watching out for me: Dominique, Eve, José, Nate, Kevin, Ana, Demetrius, Casera, Nick, Alyssa, Rachel, Caleb, Aisling, E'mon, Jasmine, Kamaria, Matt, Britteney, Raych, Aricka, Kush, Fati, Toaster, Tasha, Kaina, Sen, Adam, Dr.Camea, Natalie, Natasha, Billie, Steffen, and the Bey Family.

To the ones who believed in these poems even when I didn't: Eve, Fati, Danez, Nate, Hanif, Kevin, Franny, José, and E'mon.

To my heroes: Patricia Smith, Krista Franklin, Mahogany Browne, Noname, avery r. young, Sharon Olds, Gwendolyn Brooks, Eve Ewing, Sufjan Stevens, Solange Knowles, Joan Baez, Moses Sumney, Joanna Newsom, Rico Nasty, Fiona Apple, Mitski, and Megan Thee Stallion.

Thank you to my dearest friends. To the most wonderful Maya who is my angel, To Kyndall who is my cowboy in crime and my midwestern hero, to Ari my husband, the Lotus brothers who have my heart on a string, Georgia who is the sun, Noah who always makes art more exciting for me. Thank you Bomb Squad. Thank you Jalen, Sammy, Leah, Morgan, Lily, Emily, Selah, Camille, Lena, Ethel, Leah K. , Annilee, Amanda, Sara, and many, many more.

Thank you Pat Frazier, my best friend, my sibling. Thank you for being my fiercest believer and my fiercest challenger; for egging these poems on and for nudging me forward when I wanted to stand still. Thank you for standing by my side even when I stink.

The biggest thank you to Jamila Woods, for helping these poems learn to walk. I am so grateful for you for guiding me over these last few years. *BLOODSTONE COWBOY* is a consequence of your patience, your edits, and your care. I could not ask for a better mentor and a better role model. Cheers to you always.

about the author.

kara jackson is the daughter of country folks. She is the 2019 National Youth Poet Laureate and the 2018 Youth Poet Laureate of Chicago Her work investigates a trail of language that leads from the South to the North. Through a multidisciplinary approach, Jackson attempts to document her lineage of divine womanhood in a country that demands its erasure. She is a product of the literary bloodline created by women like Zora Neale Hurston, Toni Morrison, Alice Walker, Buffy Sainte-Marie, and Joan Baez. Jackson is an alum of the solo voice jazz ensemble at Merit School of Music. Jackson received the Scholastic Art and Writing Award for her short story *Nursery Rhymes*, which won a silver medal at the national level. She is an Adroit Journal mentee. Jackson is an alum of the Spoken Word Club at Oak Park River Forest High school. She represented the school in the Louder Than a Bomb festival from 2016-2018, and in her final year performed on final stage at the Auditorium Theatre, where she was granted the Literary Award by Patricia Smith. Her poems have appeared in *POETRY*, *Frontier Poetry*, *Rookie Mag*, *Nimrod Literary Journal*, and *Saint Heron*. She has two articles published in *Blavity*. She has two poems featured in the latest anthology edited by Kevin Coval, *The End of Chiraq*. Jackson is a TEDx speaker. She will attend Smith College in the fall of 2019.

about haymarket books.

Haymarket Books is a radical, independent, nonprofit book publisher based in Chicago.

Our mission is to publish books that contribute to struggles for social and economic justice. We strive to make our books a vibrant and organic part of social movements and the education and development of a critical, engaged, international left.

We take inspiration and courage from our namesakes, the Haymarket martyrs, who gave their lives fighting for a better world. Their 1886 struggle for the eight-hour day—which gave us May Day, the international workers' holiday—reminds workers around the world that ordinary people can organize and struggle for their own liberation. These struggles continue today across the globe—struggles against oppression, exploitation, poverty, and war.

Since our founding in 2001, Haymarket Books has published more than five hundred titles. Radically independent, we seek to drive a wedge into the risk-averse world of corporate book publishing. Our authors include Noam Chomsky, Arundhati Roy, Rebecca Solnit, Angela Y. Davis, Howard Zinn, Amy Goodman, Wallace Shawn, Mike Davis, Winona LaDuke, Ilan Pappé, Richard Wolff, Dave Zirin, Keeanga-Yamahtta Taylor, Nick Turse, Dahr Jamail, David Barsamian, Elizabeth Laird, Amira Hass, Mark Steel, Avi Lewis, Naomi Klein, and Neil Davidson. We are also the trade publishers of the acclaimed Historical Materialism Book Series and of Dispatch Books.